T0005060

IT HAPPENED TO ME

Being

HOMELESS

Stories from Survivors

SARAH EASON AND KAREN LATCHANA KENNEY

CHERITON
CHILDREN'S BOOKS

Please visit our website, www.cheritonchildrensbooks.com to see more of our high-quality books.

First Edition

Published in 2022 by Cheriton Children's Books
PO Box 7258, Bridgnorth, Shropshire, WV16 9ET, UK

© 2022 Cheriton Children's Books

Authors: Sarah Eason and Karen Latchana Kenney
Designer: Paul Myerscough
Illustrator: Sylwia Filipczak
Editor: Jennifer Sanderson
Picture Researcher: Rachel Blount
Proofreader: Tracey Kelly

Picture credits: Cover: Sylwia Filipczak; Inside: p1: Shutterstock/Ajdin Kamber; p4: Shutterstock/Roman Bodnarchuk; p6: Shutterstock/Photographee.eu; p7: Shutterstock/Taras Chaban; p8: Shutterstock/ChameleonsEye; p10: Shutterstock/ Robert J Daveant; p11: Shutterstock/Skyward Kick Productions; p12: Shutterstock/ Dusan Petkovic; p14: Shutterstock/Rawpixel.com; p15: Shutterstock/LightField Studios; p16: Shutterstock/Ajdin Kamber; p18: Shutterstock/Michael Jung; p21: Shutterstock/Fizkes; p22: Shutterstock/Twinsterphoto; p25: Shutterstock/ Followtheflow; p26: Shutterstock/Teerachai_P; p27: Shutterstock/Lolly; p28: Shutterstock/Lopolo; p30: Shutterstock/Monkey Business Images; p31: Shutterstock/ Vlue; p32: Shutterstock/AlessandroBiascioli; p35: Shutterstock/Kan_chana; p36: Shutterstock/Cameron Whitman; p37: Shutterstock/Sirtravelalot; p38: Shutterstock/ Addkm; p39: Shutterstock/Monkey Business Images; p40: Shutterstock/Yakobchuk Viacheslav; p43: Shutterstock/Alex Gorins; p45: Shutterstock/Hugo_34.

All rights reserved. No part of this book may be reproduced in any form without permission from the publisher, except by a reviewer.

Printed in the United States of America

Publisher's Note: The stories in this book are fictional stories based on extensive research of real-life experiences.

CONTENTS

CHAPTER ONE

WHEN A PERSON IS HOMELESS

In cities and towns across the United States, people experience homelessness every day. Many people see homeless men and women on the streets, but they walk past them as if they are invisible. Homelessness is a problem Americans have become used to seeing. However, it is a problem that is not going away and one that affects thousands of people each year.

WHAT IS HOMELESSNESS?

Homelessness is simply not having a home: Some homeless people might stay under a bridge or in a tent for shelter, but not every homeless person lives on the streets. For example, a homeless person can find shelter in the homes of friends or relatives; however, that shelter is not permanent, and staying there is a temporary solution. That person is still technically considered homeless.

Homelessness can happen to anyone: Every year, many young people find themselves homeless.

Being homeless makes it very difficult for people to get their basic needs met. Hunger is a constant problem, and injury and illness are serious threats. Finding food, water, shelter, and warmth become the most important things to someone on the streets. Daily life is a struggle to survive. Homelessness affects society, families, teenagers, and young children—it is an issue that cannot be ignored.

WHO BECOMES HOMELESS?

All ages and types of people can become homeless, and it can happen to almost anyone. Homelessness has many causes. Sometimes, the loss of a job causes a family to become homeless—one paycheck can mean the difference between having or not having a home. Sometimes, domestic violence is the cause of homelessness—women and their children may leave the family home to escape violence and become homeless as a result. Mental illness and **substance abuse** are other causes. There are even more reasons why people find themselves homeless.

It Happened to Me

This book follows the "It Happened to Me" fictional journals of different young people who have become homeless. These stories from survivors explain what it is like to be homeless and how it happened to them. The conclusions to their stories on pages 44-45 also show that it is possible to break free from homelessness and lead a happy and fulfilling life. The stories and information in this book can support people who are homeless and help everyone better understand what it is like to be in this situation.

NOT THE WHOLE STORY

A common **stereotype** about homeless people is that they are drug **addicts** or people who have mental health issues. While this is true for many people experiencing **chronic homelessness** and may also be the cause of their homelessness, according to the National Alliance to End Homelessness, the chronic homeless make up around just 27 percent of all homeless people. That proves that this stereotype is not a true representation of most homeless people in the United States.

SUDDEN CHANGES

People become homeless for many reasons. Poverty or some kind of financial crisis are two major reasons. For example, a job loss can cause missed rent or mortgage payments. And even if a person is working full time but only making the minimum wage, they most likely cannot afford the rent required to house an entire family. If a medical emergency or the sudden death of a family member occurs, it can cause a family to become homeless overnight.

All kinds of issues can push a person into homelessness. Once in this situation, it can be very hard to get out of it.

Homelessness means that people have to do whatever they can to survive.

OTHER LIFE PROBLEMS

Sometimes, a person's family life is filled with **abuse** or conflict—for example, violence can force women and children to leave their homes. Divorce, sexual abuse, or neglect can cause homelessness, too. Lesbian, gay, bisexual, transgender, and queer (LGBTQ+) teenagers who come out to their parents may not be accepted—many teenagers are thrown out of their homes because of their sexuality.

Veterans are another homeless group. Some soldiers come back from war with physical **disabilities** or mental health issues, and as a result, it becomes difficult for them to maintain regular nonmilitary lives. Sometimes, these problems even lead to addiction or violence, and the veterans may lose their homes as a result.

A recent report found that four groups of people had a high risk of becoming homeless. They were people living with friends, family, or nonrelatives because they could not afford their own homes; prisoners; young adults who had become too old for **foster care**; and people who did not have health insurance.

HOMELESS FOR A SHORT TIME

Most people experience homelessness for only a short period of time, and this is called transitional homelessness. Some kind of major crisis, such as a **natural disaster**, a job loss, or a medical condition usually causes transitional homelessness. This type of crisis can lead to an individual or an entire family becoming homeless. One US Conference of Mayors report found that a lack of affordable housing was the leading cause of homelessness for families with children. Poverty, unemployment, eviction (forcing someone from their home), and domestic violence were other leading causes.

Families can be forced onto the street and into transitional homelessness because they can no longer afford their housing.

"Losing my job pushed me into homelessness—I had no money, no help, and nowhere to live."

A PLACE TO STAY

If families or individuals lose their homes, they most likely will spend some time with friends or family, perhaps sleeping on couches or in spare rooms. With this support, they can work and save money to get back into their own homes again. Without friends or family to offer a place to stay, some people have nowhere to go. These temporarily homeless people may sleep in their cars for awhile or find a place that offers transitional housing. Wherever they stay, people who are temporarily homeless usually find permanent housing within a year of becoming homeless. Homeless people such as these require temporary housing for only a short period of time until they are able to support themselves once again.

IT HAPPENED TO THEM

Transitional housing isn't just a place to stay: Most transitional housing centers offer services that help people overcome their financial difficulties. Twenty-one-year-old Millie became homeless when living with her boyfriend and his family during a Covid-19 lockdown. Millie and her boyfriend's family argued, until she felt forced to move out of their home. Millie sofa-surfed until the workers at a transitional housing center helped her. They moved her into sheltered housing and helped her with her finances. With their support, Millie was able to buy the equipment that she needed to go back to college and continue her studies.

LONG-TERM HOMELESSNESS

People who are chronically homeless have very different needs to people who are temporarily homeless. They need more than just a little time to get back on their feet, and to stay in permanent housing, they may need help for the remainder of their lives.

Many people who are chronically homeless have a serious mental illness, a substance addiction, or a physical disability. They could be suffering from schizophrenia, which is a brain disorder that causes voices in a person's head and feelings of **paranoia**, making it difficult for a person with this disorder to function in daily life. A chronically homeless person may have a severe addiction problem or a physical disability, which could also prevent them from holding down a job and paying their bills. These are not problems that can be easily fixed.

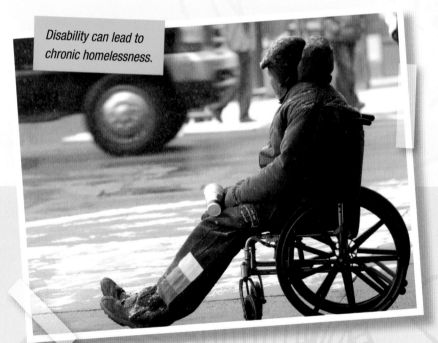

Disability can lead to chronic homelessness.

Many people who are chronically homeless have a serious mental illness ...

Unfortunately, for many people on the streets, jail is the only shelter they will find.

THE HOMELESS CYCLE

The chronically homeless may spend decades going from hospitals to emergency shelters to living on the streets. They cycle through different programs and treatments, ending back on the streets once more. They may even end up in jail. These people require permanent housing help and other types of support to end their cycle of homelessness.

According to the National Alliance to End Homelessness, 11.8 percent of the US population lives in poverty and struggles to afford necessities such as food and housing. In 2018, 6.5 million Americans spent more than 50 percent of their income on housing, leaving them with money for little else and in serious financial difficulty.

This Could Happen to Anyone

FRIDAY JANUARY 15

Dad came home from work early. I can't believe he's being laid off. He says it's not just him but most of his office. I always thought his job was safe. He says not to worry—he and Mom have savings. Plus, he thinks he'll get hired right away. But I am freaking out. Last night on CBS, it sounded like the economy is really bad. At dinner, both of them were kinda making a joke of it. I think they are putting on a brave face. Jaden says I always overreact. He says listen to Mom and Dad.

MONDAY APRIL 5

I talked to Mrs. Bergmann after school today. She says I should be preparing for SATs because she thinks I've got a shot at an Ivy League school! Then she asked if things are OK. I know it's because my GPA has fallen. Didn't want to tell her just what was going on, so I just said everything was fine. It's too embarrassing to tell her that Dad has stopped paying the mortgage and can't find a job.

I never thought that I'd end up living in a motel.

WEDNESDAY MAY 12

We've been at Aunt Ellie's for a week now. We had to move in after the mortgage company **repossessed** the house. We had nowhere else to go. Have started getting to school early. If I'm in by 6.30 a.m., I can use the shower without anyone noticing. There are just too many of us at Ellie's. It's so great that she's letting us stay, but I can tell that she and Mom have been arguing and I'm worried she might ask us to leave. I know Uncle Mike doesn't want us ...

THURSDAY SEPTEMBER 2

Who would have thought I would be a sophomore living in a motel? Things came to a head with Uncle Mike, just like I knew they would. He kept talking about how great his job was and how secure it was. You could see how angry it made Dad—he went crazy and said we were going. We had to pack our bags and go to a motel, but it is way, way worse than Aunt Ellie's. Now we can only afford ONE room, so all four of us are squashed in. Dad is **depressed**. Nobody is hiring mortgage brokers. Mom's applied for a part-time job at Target. She says they're the only ones hiring.

TUESDAY OCTOBER 19

Mrs. Bergmann asked me to stay behind after math class today. She wanted to know why my grades are up and down all the time. She said if they kept going on like this, med school would never happen. I broke down. I told her how bad it had been; that we were living in a motel and that I have no place to study. When the school library is shut, I have no quiet place to go. The motel is so noisy. She totally got what I was saying, she said this could happen to anyone and it's not my fault. She told me she would talk to the principal. For the first time in months, I feel a little better about everything ...

TEENS AND HOMELESSNESS

Teenagers on the street are incredibly vulnerable: They need help to survive because the street is a dangerous environment for anyone, let alone a teenager. Homeless teens become easy targets for adult **predators**, who can offer food, money, or a bed to sleep in. However, the consequences of this can be sexual, mental, and physical abuse. With such serious consequences, why would teenagers leave the safety of a home for the streets?

Problems at home can push a teenager onto the streets.

Establishing an accurate count of homeless teenagers is difficult because most try to stay hidden from the authorities. However, knowing their numbers helps the organizations that provide services to homeless people understand their needs. National homelessness counts range between 600,000 to 1.6 million each year.

UNHAPPY HOMES

Many teenagers leave home because they do not come from safe and supportive homes to begin with. Many have problems within their families—for example, there may be sexual or physical abuse in their home or domestic violence between parents. Substance abuse by a parent or mental illness may be other causes of abuse, and these problems may result in the neglect of the children in the home. A parent's job or home loss may also cause the teen's homelessness.

Parents may reject their LGBTQ+ children when they come out, and these teenagers may then be forced to leave their homes because of their sexuality. According to one report, almost 40 percent of homeless young people are LGBTQ+ youth.

LACK OF SUPPORT

The foster, **juvenile justice**, and mental health systems often fail to support young people. These systems support teenagers only until they turn 18, after which they must go into the world and care for themselves, regardless of their financial or basic life skills.

Many LGBTQ+ young people find their families do not accept them and even ask them to leave home.

LIFE ON THE STREET

Once they leave home, teenagers must quickly learn to adapt and deal with life on the streets. Not having a home makes the simplest of things much more difficult—for example, homeless teenagers must carry all their necessities with them at all times because they have no permanent place to store their clothes, blankets, toiletries, or any other personal items they own. Finding a dry, warm, and safe place to sleep is another immediate concern. Teenagers might sleep under bridges, in tents, or in abandoned garages or houses. However, these are not safe places to sleep, so some teenagers try to sleep during the day, when it is less likely they may be attacked. At night, they stay awake, walking the streets.

Searching for food among garbage may be the only option for homeless teenagers who are desperately hungry.

In order for some teens to have enough money to buy food, they turn to prostitution, sometimes willingly but at other times, they are pushed into it by adults. According to the National Sexual Violence Resource Center (NSVRC), one in three teens who are living on the street will be lured into prostitution within 48 hours of leaving home. The Center reports that 82 percent will trade sex for money, and 48 percent trade sex for food or a place to stay.

IT HAPPENS

Most homeless teenagers have difficulty finding employment. They may not be old enough to work or be suitable for different jobs, and maintaining a job while sleeping on the streets may become impossible. Instead, to have money for food, many homeless young people "panhandle," which is asking strangers to give them money. It can be humiliating for homeless people to panhandle, but it is a last resort in order to be able to buy food. Some people argue that panhandling should be made illegal because they believe that it is a public nuisance.

GOING HUNGRY, KEEPING CLEAN

Food and water are two constant concerns for homeless teenagers. If teenagers have money, they may be able to buy food. However, many do not and rely on strangers to give them food. These young people may also search for unused or leftover food that has been thrown in the garbage at restaurants. Some desperate teenagers even steal food from stores. Homeless young people do not have easy access to bathrooms or showers, so it becomes difficult for them to stay clean and wash their clothes. Being unclean is a problem in itself, because it can lead to a number of health issues.

"I was scared all the time on the streets."

SAFETY AT SCHOOL

School can be the one place homeless teenagers find stability, and many continue to go to school despite their desperate situation. According to data released by the National Center for Homeless Education (NCHE), in the 2017–2018 school year, there were 1.5 million children and youth in public schools who were identified as experiencing homelessness.

FACING CHALLENGES IN THE CLASSROOM

School poses its own problems for homeless students. Most homeless teens don't want other students to know that they are homeless, so they work hard to hide it from their friends to avoid being bullied or teased. Being homeless also makes it difficult for teens to maintain their studies—if they do not have a place to study, they will most likely fall behind with their homework and grades. Since they may not have a safe place to sleep, they come to school exhausted, sometimes falling asleep in class or struggling to concentrate. Without access to transportation, it may also be difficult for them to get to school. In addition to all this, the stress of being homeless affects their ability to do schoolwork.

Homeless students may suffer emotionally and academically because of their situation.

IT HAPPENED TO THEM

Fifteen-year-old Adele suffered from anxiety, or extreme worry, from the age of 11 due to bullying at school. As a result, she began to skip school, and her problems then worsened when she began to argue with her mom. Feeling unable to cope, Adele sofa-surfed for awhile, staying with her sister until she eventually sought help from a housing center. Its workers helped Adele find housing and supported her with counseling. Adele has since been able to repair her relationship with her mother.

IT ALL ADDS UP

A homeless teen's substantial problems all add up. They affect how well they do in school, and over time, being homeless can seriously affect a student's achievement. Students can develop learning problems and have literacy and numeracy skills. If these problems are not addressed, these students leave school without the skills needed to succeed, and they may fail to get jobs and become independent adults who can support themselves.

Teachers and school counselors can offer help to homeless teenagers by informing them of available community services. Some schools offer special services for their homeless students, including shower facilities, meals, clean clothes, and extended after-school activities.

I Never Thought This Would Happen

THURSDAY AUGUST 19

It is sooooo hot! Mom said Florida was hot in the summer, but I was not expecting it to be a total sweat fest. It is so not like Wisconsin. It kinda feels like being on vacation all the time. Don't like the bugs, though. They are huge! But I am glad we are here and that Mom finally took control. The last few months were pretty scary. Dan was being an idiot, and I think he was **using** again. Him selling Mom's necklace—the one Grandma left her—was the final straw. Thank God we left.

SUNDAY SEPTEMBER 12

Things are OK. My new high school is alright, but I have a ton of homework. I know I am behind. I shouldn't have missed all those classes last year, but things were so hard at home that it was easier not to go. I'm trying to fit in—some of the girls are a little too preppy, and most of the guys are jocks. But, hey, it's only been a couple of weeks. The best news is that we moved into our new apartment! It only has two bedrooms, so I have to share with Cindy and Meghan, but that's OK. Mom even got a job, so she's going to treat us to Denny's!

WEDNESDAY JANUARY 12

Why does Mom always do this? She just can't be on her own. And she can't see that she keeps doing the same thing. Over and over. Like a broken record. Her latest is Joel. TBH, Joel is a loser. I didn't like him the minute she brought him back. He was trying to be super-nice, especially to Meghan because she's the baby. It was so fake, but I could see right through him. I don't like the way he talks to Mom.

FRIDAY FEBRUARY 11

Things are sooo bad again. Valentine's Day was a total joke yesterday—Mom told us Joel is going to move in with us—he's lost his place, and she says he has nowhere to go. Then she said now we can be like a new family! How many times have we heard that?! He's already hit her, though she denies it. Today, I told him to quit hassling Mom, and he got real nasty with me. Waited until Mom was out the room, then he said he would make me pay. I really don't like Joel, and I don't want to be here.

WEDNESDAY MARCH 23

I've left home—I just walked out. I couldn't stand it anymore. Joel kept threatening me, and I just know he's still hitting Mom, even though she said he stopped. I don't know what to do—or where I'll go.

I just need some time to clear my head and think about what to do next. I am scared, but I'm more scared of what will happen if I stay. I can't believe I've had to leave with nowhere to go. I never thought this would happen to me ...

When I walked out, I just went and sat in the park. I couldn't believe that things had gotten so bad.

CHAPTER THREE

LIFE ON THE STREETS

The longer a teenager remains homeless, the more likely it is that homelessness will have serious health effects. It is physically demanding to be homeless. Without shelter, young people are exposed to harsh weather and temperatures. They may get frostbite, or injury to the body's tissues from exposure to extreme cold, or have wounds that do not heal fully. Being exposed can weaken people's **immune systems**. They are likely to get sick more often than housed teenagers, contracting **bronchitis**, **pneumonia**, or other illnesses. Homeless teenagers are also less likely to seek or receive medical care because they are worried that if they are discovered to be homeless, they will be returned to the families they have run away from or forced into foster care.

Being homeless can cause serious long-term health issues.

DRUGS ON THE STREET

Teenagers are also exposed to drug use while on the streets. They may have used before they were homeless, or they may start while homeless. Some use drugs to cope with the stress and anxiety that comes with living on the streets, however, the drugs just end up making their problems worse. For some, the use turns to addiction, and an addiction can make it even harder for teenagers to find permanent housing or a job. Dealing with an addiction usually also requires medical help, because coming off drugs is a difficult process for most people. It is even more difficult for a homeless person, who struggles to meet their basic needs every day. Addiction of any form also brings its own set of health issues.

IT HAPPENS

A recent survey concluded that approximately 30 percent of people who are chronically homeless have mental health conditions, and more than 60 percent of those who are chronically homeless have experienced mental health problems throughout their lives. The facts around homelessness and substance abuse follow a similar trend. Around 50 percent of homeless people have substance abuse issues, and more than 80 percent have experienced lifetime alcohol and/or drug problems.

It is physically demanding to be homeless.

FEELING INVISIBLE

Being homeless can make people feel invisible to society: Many people look past the homeless, as if they cannot see them. Homeless people can start to feel disconnected from society—as if they don't even belong to it anymore. It is important to remember that anyone can become homeless. This is a reality that most people don't want to face, so they choose to ignore it instead. However, feeling invisible and ignored can be emotionally difficult for homeless people and can wear down their **self-esteem**.

The feelings of alienation from society are why homeless teenagers try to connect with others on the street. It also helps to be part of a group, so that the teens are less vulnerable to dangerous adults. Homeless young

IT HAPPENS

A hate crime is an act of violence against a person or group of people based on someone's hatred for that type of person or group. Some people target the homeless for hate crimes, including beatings, rapes, and setting people on fire. In just one year, the National Coalition for the Homeless recorded that hate crimes killed 32 homeless people. Teenagers and young men committed nearly all of the attacks.

"I felt like I wasn't really there— no one seemed to see me anymore."

People often walk past homeless people as if they do not exist. This makes the homeless feel invisible and that they are no longer important in society.

people create street families—friendships with other, more experienced homeless teenagers. The more experienced teenagers teach the less experienced how to survive. They protect each other, but the protection usually comes at a price. These families may have abusive and unhealthy types of relationships that involve sex and substance abuse.

USING SEX TO SURVIVE

Survival sex is one common problem with homeless young people. Many trade sex for food, clothes, money, or drugs. Most teenagers do not have money to buy what they need and do not want to go to shelters, so they believe that sex is the most valuable thing they can trade. However, this sexual trade targets vulnerable young people and can have terrible results. Teenagers may contract **sexually transmitted diseases** or find themselves with unwanted pregnancies.

While living on the streets, in shelters, or searching for housing, LGBTQ+ homeless teens are more likely to endure traumatic, or very upsetting, experiences. These include harassment and abuse from **peers** and shelter staff, as a result of their **sexual orientation** and/or **gender expression**.

25

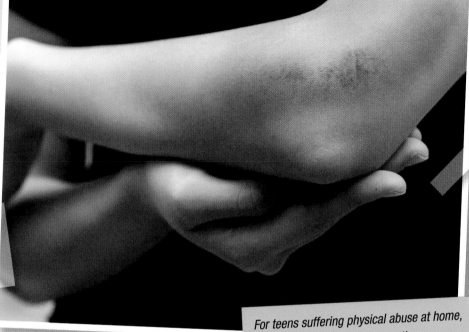

For teens suffering physical abuse at home, the street can seem a safer option.

ESCAPING TO THE STREET

Young people may leave home because they are being sexually or physically abused. They escape to the streets, but there they are at risk of even more abuse. According to the National Network for Youth (NN4Y), homeless young people are two to three times more likely to be raped or assaulted than other youth.

LOOKING FOR THE YOUNG

Predatory adults look for young people alone on the streets. These teenagers are vulnerable and scared, and therefore, they are much easier for an adult to target than a teen in a safe environment. Predatory adults are adults who try to find young people that they can lure to come with them to another place. They may promise homeless teenagers food, clothing, or money. They give them attention and may even tell them that they are special or loved. However, the predatory adults are not trying to help these teenagers—instead, they usually want to sexually or physically abuse them. These predatory adults may be pimps, drug dealers, criminals, or people who seem ordinary.

MENTAL SUFFERING

Many homeless youth also have a mental illness. They develop emotional problems, such as depression and **post-traumatic stress disorder (PTSD)**, as a result of their difficult experiences. They do not know how to deal with their physical or sexual abuse. They have anxiety or high levels of stress, constantly worried about finding food or shelter. They also worry about being assaulted by strangers. Their mental illness may lead them to attempt suicide. Most do not receive medication or **therapy** to help with their illnesses.

A homeless teen who is alone is vulnerable to predatory adults.

A 2020 article published in *Psychiatric Times* revealed that there is a link between homelessness and psychiatric disorders, but there are several factors that may keep homeless people from seeking the psychiatric help they need. These include lack of money, limited transportation, and the illness itself. They also include the homeless putting basic needs, such as food, clean water, and shelter, before their mental well-being.

27

I've Lost Everything I Ever Had

MONDAY DECEMBER 27

Grandma and I had just the best-ever Xmas since Mom passed. Grandma got me an iPhone! I can't believe it. How did she manage to keep it hidden for so long? She said she'd been saving for months, and then she got Linda to go get it for her. Linda is the coolest neighbor ever! I don't think Grandma has left the neighborhood since I started junior high. She says the Loop is just full of fancy people now, and she is staying put! I love Grandma, I am so lucky to have her.

THURSDAY JUNE 16

Grandma is gone. I can't believe it. She passed away, just like that. One minute we were sitting watching television, then she just slumped in her chair. I didn't know what to do. I screamed out and ran down the hall to Linda. She called 911, but it was too late. Now, **Social Services** are saying I can't stay here on my own. I said Linda would take care of me, but they said no—until I turn 16, I have to go live with a foster family. But I said I don't know any foster families. They said they will find me a nice family who will take care of me. Now I am just waiting. I'm really scared.

If Grandma was still alive, she'd never have let this happen to me. She was all the family I had.

SUNDAY JULY 4

This the first 4th of July I've ever spent without Grandma. I am living with a family named the Hyatts. They have two kids—Drew is older than me. He's 17 and Amy is 12. They have everything. They have a yard with a basketball hoop, soccer nets, and even a trampoline. Everyone is super friendly, but it is weird—and it's not Grandma's. Everyone here is really rich. It's a really nice neighborhood, but I feel like everyone is looking at me all the time and wondering where I came from. I wonder what Grandma would have said. She'd tell me to be polite. I am being polite, but I feel like people don't get me.

WEDNESDAY SEPTEMBER 21

I have tried really hard to like my new school. But I hate it. Everyone is so fake. They pretend that I'm the same as them, but then they say things like "My dad says poor people are just lazy." They don't know how lucky there are to have a family. At lunch, I usually sit on my own. Drew says hello, but he hangs out with his soccer crowd, and I can tell he doesn't want them to know he knows me. I have no one to talk to. Mr. and Mrs. Hyatt don't understand how I feel, although they are always asking me if I am OK and telling me to talk to them. But ... I just can't.

SATURDAY OCTOBER 22

I've left the Hyatts. I packed my stuff and left before anyone was up. I had to walk a mile to the nearest bus stop. It's taken me all day to get back to the city. I thought I would stay with Linda, but she's not at home. No one knows if she's left town. I was gonna call her, but my phone's out of credit. I don't know what to do. I am hungry, and I don't know where I will sleep tonight. I have a few dollars, but that's all I've lost everything I ever had.

CHAPTER FOUR

HELPING THE HOMELESS

Organizations provide different services to assist homeless teenagers—for example, some have van or street outreach programs in which members of the organization go to the streets to find homeless young people. Once the homeless are identified, some of the outreach program workers may offer them food. Others seek out young people to let them know what services their organization provides and where they can get a warm meal and clean clothes.

OFFERING HELP

Homeless shelters provide short-term services to homeless teenagers. There, homeless youth can find a bed for the night and free meals, and they can take a shower and possibly get some clean clothes. Teenagers can also talk with counselors who try to understand why these young people are homeless, offering advice or information to help them. The counselors may also help the teenagers reconnect with their families.

Many homeless shelters provide food for people during holidays, such as Christmas.

Outreach workers look for homeless teenagers sleeping rough to try and help them find shelter and safety.

CONTINUING HELP

Transitional housing helps homeless teenagers for longer periods of time. Homeless young people can continue with counseling and get help with their education. They can learn life skills, receive medical care, and also get help finding a job. The goal of transitional housing is to help homeless young people live independently. Different organizations focus on certain needs, such as teenagers who have addictions or single teenage mothers. Permanent supportive housing is also available for homeless young people. It is generally for the chronically homeless who will need support for their entire lives—they pay a small percentage of their rent, and government funding pays the remainder.

According to the US Department of Housing and Urban Development (HUD), in 2020, more people who were experiencing homelessness were unsheltered than were sheltered. California alone accounted for more than half of the country's unsheltered homeless people.

LEARNING NEW SKILLS

Some programs help teenagers develop specific skills, such as art or job skills. For example, one café in Grand Junction, Colorado, helps homeless teenagers gain valuable job experience. The café is called Café V, and it has partnered with a homeless shelter for teenagers. The vegetarian café hires teenagers from the shelter, giving them work opportunities that might otherwise be hard to find. Butter Bakery and Café, in Minneapolis, Minnesota, partners with local services to provide jobs and mentor at-risk young people. These types of programs give homeless teenagers job training and boost their self-esteem.

Art, such as legal graffiti, is a great way for people to express themselves.

USING ART THERAPY

Another great way to connect with homeless young people is through art. ArtStart is one program in New York City. It holds daily workshops for homeless young people, in which local artists and teachers volunteer their time to develop art and music projects with homeless teenagers. The young people work on their artistic skills and also develop relationships with their mentors. Art can be an amazing tool through which to express a person's feelings, which is something that may be extremely difficult for homeless teenagers to do.

Different programs have a lot to offer homeless teenagers. However, many teenagers avoid programs in an attempt to stay hidden, afraid that they will be forced to go into foster care or back to abusive homes. By connecting with young people via their passions, such as art or music, programs can more easily reach vulnerable young people and deliver their services to them.

IT HAPPENS

Almost 20,000 young people age out of foster care in the United States each year. Many have not completed high school or do not have a general education degree (GED).

"When I paint, I feel like I escape. I'm not on the streets anymore."

Punished for Being Myself

FRIDAY JANUARY 1

New Year. Dad says we have to work extra shifts in the restaurant because it's fully booked for the holidays. I told him I had other plans. I didn't tell him what those plans are—to party with Kai! She's been keeping my makeup at her place, ready for the party. Kai says it's safe there since she'll never use it! Kai's lucky. Her parents totally get that she's trans, and they are so supportive. Can't imagine telling Dad about me ...

TUESDAY JANUARY 5

I have been grounded! I'll be 18 soon, and Dad still treats me like I am 10. He was furious that I skipped the last hour of the shift. I went to the party with Kai. It was great. I wore my makeup, and everyone said I looked amazing. Plus, I met a guy who is trans, just like me—Doug. We planned to meet after the party, but I had to tell him I couldn't make it. Didn't tell him I was grounded, I'm not that dumb!

MONDAY MAY 3

Dad and I had another fight. I finally snapped and told him about me being trans. I told him I know it will be hard, but that is who I really am. He went crazy. Started shouting that I was just trying to ruin his business and reputation. Then Mom got hysterical. I couldn't take it, so I stormed out and went to Doug's. He totally gets that I am not happy as I am.

THURSDAY MAY 13

Another fight at home. I can't take any more of Dad's transgender hate. Doug says it's OK to stay with him. Doug is 25, but you wouldn't think so. One minute he's acting like he's 15, and the next, he's the serious tech guy making loads of dollars! Doug says it's hard being trans and that we need to stick together.

He says I only have one more year of education left, then my life can really begin. If my grades hold up, I should get to college—and be free.

FRIDAY OCTOBER 8

Doug said he's really sorry, but he is moving to another city with his job. That means I can't keep living with him. Doug says he is worried about me—where will I go? I said, don't worry, I'll figure something out. But I'm scared. I know I can't go back home, and I don't have anywhere else to go. I can't tell Doug that, though. It's not fair to worry him.

FRIDAY OCTOBER 29

I moved out of Doug's today. He flies out tomorrow to his new job. Told Doug I am going to stay with Kai, but that's a lie. I know her folks don't have room there for me—their apartment is tiny. There is no one I can stay with. What am I going to do? I can't call Mom. I haven't talked to her since the spring. During that last row, I said some really bad stuff, and Dad was horrible.

I have nowhere to go. I still have months left of school. I want to graduate. And I want to start being the real me, but how's that going happen if I have no place to live? I feel like I'm being punished for being myself.

I can't help feeling the way I do. I'm homeless just because of who I am.

CHAPTER FIVE

STOPPING THE CYCLE

The problem of homelessness is growing, and some cities are responding with law enforcement. In these cases, laws that target the activities of homeless people are brought into force, making it illegal to sleep, eat, sit, and panhandle in public spaces. Homeless people can then be arrested if found breaking these laws. Many cities employ extra officers to enforce the laws—they hope that the laws will drive homeless people from their cities. According to the National Coalition for the Homeless, some of the toughest laws targeting homeless people are found in Sarasota, Florida, and Lawrence, Kansas. There, it is illegal to sleep outdoors and panhandle.

A homeless person can be arrested in certain states for lingering on the streets or asking for money.

ENDING UP IN JAIL

The results of homelessness laws are that homeless people end up in the **criminal justice system**. They spend time in jail and have criminal records, which can be especially damaging to young people who are placed in jails with tough criminals. Some people believe arresting homeless people is not a solution to the problem at all. If anything, it just makes the problem worse because a criminal record makes it even harder for a homeless person to find employment or housing. The costs of the justice system are also higher than the costs of providing supportive housing. Is it right to arrest someone for not having a home? Many people believe it isn't and believe that it is an attack on a homeless person's civil rights.

Once arrested, teens may enter the justice system and gain criminal records.

Studies of people in jail who were homeless before their imprisonment show that many had mental health issues and had experienced very traumatic situations. Seventy-five percent of previously homeless prisoners had a mental illness, 49 percent had been attacked with a knife or another sharp weapon, and 31 percent had been physically or sexually abused.

HELPING THE HOMELESS

Communities recognize that homelessness is a growing problem, which is why there are many services available for the homeless. These services are offered at the local, state, and national levels. Many churches and **nonprofit** organizations run programs to help the homeless. Individuals in communities donate to these charities, giving clothing, money, or food, then the charities distribute the goods to those in need. Some services help a person who is at risk of becoming homeless by providing small **grants** to help with mortgage or rent payments. Charities and organizations also run shelters, housing facilities, medical clinics, and food banks. The United Way is one large organization that provides funding for local and national programs that help the homeless.

Providing food is just one of the ways that organizations help homeless people.

HELPING FURTHER

Federal funding comes from a variety of sources. For example, the McKinney-Vento Homeless Assistance Grants program provides funding for homeless programs across the country—it is the largest funding program for the homeless in the United States. The program emphasizes help for homeless families with children, homelessness prevention, and permanent supportive housing. The Homelessness Prevention and Rapid Re-Housing program also funds local and state programs. Its focus is on prevention and helping people move from shelters to independent living. There are several other federal programs that also fund different types of services.

Programs can provide counseling to help young people in trouble and keep them from becoming homeless.

IT HAPPENS

Operation Stand Down Rhode Island is a community program that provides services for homeless veterans in the state. The program gives rental assistance and has housing facilities as part of its services.

PREVENTING HOMELESSNESS

Prevention is one key factor to ending homelessness. Prevention for adults can mean receiving money to help with rent or mortgage payments during difficult times—a family can become homeless after missing just one of these payments. With small grants, families gain time to find work or figure out a plan to keep them from losing their homes.

Help and advice at an early stage can help a parent work through their problems so that they avoid homelessness.

Studies can throw light on the problem of homelessness and help educate people about the problem. For example, they can show how race and gender have a part to play. One study carried out in New York City and Philadelphia showed that their chronically homeless populations were mainly black and male. In New York City, 92.2 percent were black and 83.3 were male. In Philadelphia, 92.9 percent were black and 71.1 percent were male.

WORKING WITH FAMILIES

For teenagers, prevention may come in the form of intervention from a counselor or child welfare worker. If families are fighting, therapy may help solve their problems, and in cases of neglect or abuse, a child welfare worker can place a teenager or child in a safer situation.

Parents can also be educated about being more involved with their children's lives. For example, if substance abuse is affecting them, with education, parents may be better able to notice the signs and offer help that will prevent children from running away and becoming homeless.

GETTING A MESSAGE ACROSS

The media is also a powerful tool for educating the public. For example, the Spare Some Change media campaign focuses on the street youth in Los Angeles. Through documentaries, public service announcements, street teams, and social media, the program spreads awareness of youth homelessness and connects homeless teenagers with people who can help them. This is just one of many media campaigns aimed at educating the public about homelessness to try and help prevent the problem.

IT HAPPENS

Every November, National Homeless Youth Awareness Month events are held in communities around the United States. Standup For Kids and YouthLink are two organizations that help spread the word about youth homelessness during the month. These and other organizations use social media, panel discussions, and blogs to spread awareness of the size of the problem.

THE PROBLEMS CONTINUE

Homelessness can have some lasting effects on society. Without help, teenagers who are homeless can grow up to be troubled adults. They may then not reach their full potential and therefore may not be able to properly contribute to their communities.

Since homelessness usually interrupts education, a homeless young person may lag educationally behind his or her peers. This has a ripple effect that follows the teenager into adulthood. Without support, a homeless young person may not complete a high school education, and then college becomes difficult or even impossible. Without education or job training, homeless teenagers can become unemployable adults, who then add to the US unemployment rate. If these young people do manage to find jobs, they may only be those that do not pay a living wage.

IT HAPPENS

Due to hard economic times, many cities are filled with vacant, or empty, homes. Some city authorities are considering housing the homeless in those vacant homes. Some believe this would be the ideal solution to the problem of homelessness, especially since there are so many vacant homes. According to Amnesty International, there are more than five times as many vacant homes as there are homeless people in the United States.

CAUGHT IN A TRAP

If homeless young people enter the justice system because of being homeless, it can be more damaging than helpful. Many kinds of criminals are in the justice system, and once in that system, homeless young people are exposed to violence and different kinds of criminal activity. Many homeless teenagers are also treated like dangerous criminals, when they are actually very vulnerable young people. It also costs more to keep a homeless young person in jail than it costs to provide housing—one Colorado study found that it costs around $5,887 to permanently keep a youth off the streets. The study found that it cost $53,665 to keep a youth in jail for a year. Once the person leaves the justice system, it may be even harder to move back toward an independent life in society. As an adult, the homeless person may simply find themselves back in jail again. For this destructive cycle to be broken, money, time, and kindness are needed to help homeless young people turn their lives around.

Many cities have empty or disused buildings that could be turned into housing for homeless people.

New Beginnings

JAIMIE'S STORY
THURSDAY FEBRUARY 17

So much has happened in the last few months. Dad finally got a job. And it's a good job! His old boss has hired him—he's started a new company and wanted Dad on board from the get-go. It means that we now have somewhere to live that isn't that gross motel. We are renting, and Dad says that hopefully we will be able to buy again. I have my own room again (yay!). I will never not appreciate my own space ever again.

My grades are picking up again, and I feel like I have a shot at getting to med school. I want to make it there more than ever now.

RACHEL'S STORY
MONDAY APRIL 25

I am writing my diary back home. A month ago, I didn't think I would ever write those words ... But Mom finally realized what a jerk Joel is. After I left, she kept calling my cell phone. I didn't answer,

I just walked around the park, then headed downtown. I walked until I was so tired, I fell asleep on a bench outside the grocery store. The security guard woke me up. He asked me what I was doing, and why wasn't I home. Said it wasn't safe for a young girl to be out. He bought me some breakfast. I said I would call Mom. She was sobbing and said she would never put her boyfriend before her kids again. When I got back, Joel was gone. So maybe this time it will be different. I really hope so.

DAMIEN'S STORY
SATURDAY OCTOBER 29

I am back with the Hyatts. Turns out they really are looking out for me. After I left, they called the police. They put out a missing person's description of me. So when I was walking around my old neighborhood after I went looking for Linda, a police car pulled over. I nearly ran ... I thought they were going to arrest me for running away. But the cops were nice.

44

They asked who I was. At first, I didn't want to say anything, but then I started to cry and told them everything. They made some calls. I rode back to the Hyatts in the police car! That was weird. Since then, my **social worker** and the Hyatts have been talking. I am going to change school after Halloween. There's another school they think will suit me better. It's farther away, but the school bus can pick me up. It's a new beginning, Grandma would say,

DAVID'S STORY
SATURDAY NOVEMBER 20

I am back home. After I left Doug's, I just sat and cried. I didn't know what to do. Finally, I called Mom. She told me to come home, right now. Mom has been amazing—she told Dad they need to change. That they should love me no matter what. This last week they have been in touch with a parent support group for people with trans kids. They even went to a meeting. Never in a million years did I think my dad would do that! But he did, and now he says even though he still finds it hard to accept, he is starting to get why I feel like I do.

David: I'm glad I kept my journal through all this. When I read back and see how bad things were, I realize how far I've come. I know that I'll never feel that bad again.

I cried when he said that. Dad says I can keep living with him and Mom as long as I want. It feels good to hear that, but I really want to have my own space as soon as I can. I'm so happy I have college ahead of me. After years of hiding who I really am, I finally feel like I can have the future I want. I never thought that would happen—but it has.

GLOSSARY

abuse physical or emotional harm inflicted upon a person

addicts people who are unable to stop using something, such as drugs or alcohol

bronchitis inflammation of the lungs that results in coughing

chronic homelessness being homeless for at least a year

criminal justice system the system of law enforcement in which people are tried and punished for crimes

depressed having a mental illness that causes severe sadness

disabilities physical or mental conditions that limit what people can do

foster care the system of temporary care of children by adults who are not their parents

gender expression the way in which someone shows their gender identity, for example, the way that they dress

grants sums of money given by governments or organizations for a particular purpose

immune systems complicated systems in the body that fight infection

juvenile justice a system of law for young people under age 18

natural disaster a naturally occurring event on Earth that causes death and destruction, such as an earthquake

nonprofit not for profit, or monies made after all costs have been paid

paranoia unhelpful and often suspicious beliefs that are not true

peers people of a similar age

pneumonia inflammation of the lungs that can result in serious illness

post-traumatic stress disorder (PTSD) a mental disorder that some people experience after a traumatic event

predators people who seek out vulnerable people in order to use them

repossessed taken back ownership

self-esteem pride in or respect for oneself

sexual orientation a person's identity in terms of which gender they are attracted to

sexually transmitted diseases diseases that are passed to other people through sexual activity

Social Services the name for a collection of organizations that are provided for the benefit of the community and paid for by the government

social worker a person who works with social services and helps people in need

stereotype a widely held but inaccurate belief about people

substance abuse harmful or out-of-control use of a substance

therapy talking about mental health issues with a trained professional

using taking drugs regularly

veterans ex-members of the armed forces

FIND OUT MORE

BOOKS

Lusted, Marcia Amidon. *Coping with Homelessness* (Coping). Rosen Publishing, 2018.

Lusted, Marcia Amidon. *I Am Homeless. Now What?* (Teen Life 411). Rosen Publishing, 2017.

Uhl, Xina M. *Homelessness* (Rosen Verified: Current Issues). Rosen Publishing, 2021.

WEBSITES

Learn about homelessness in the United States and how to end it: **endhomelessness.org/homelessness-in-america/who-experiences-homelessness/youth**

Find out more about runaways and homelessness at: **kidshealth.org/en/teens/runaway.html?ref=search**

ORGANIZATIONS

Teen Line
Cedars-Sinai
P.O. Box 48750
Los Angeles, CA 90048
(310) 855-HOPE (4673) or
(800) TLC-TEEN (852-8336)
Website: teenlineonline.org
If you are struggling with homelessness, or know someone who is, help is out there. Connect and get support at this great help site for teenagers.

PUBLISHER'S NOTE TO EDUCATORS AND PARENTS:

All the websites featured above have been carefully reviewed to ensure that they are suitable for students. However, many websites change often, and we cannot guarantee that a site's future contents will continue to meet our high standards of educational value. Please be advised that students should be closely monitored whenever they access the Internet.

INDEX

ABOUT THE AUTHORS

Sarah Eason has authored many nonfiction books for children and has a special interest in health and social issues for young people. Karen Latchana Kenney is a well-known children's book author who has written a huge range information books for young people.